To: The Salem
The Aleph

Table of Contents

Be empowered
Bro Afuma
muHammad
8-13-15

Providing Options Publishing Company

**101 Proven and Effective Strategies
for Empowering Black Boys**

For Counselors, Social Workers, Teachers, Administrators and other Support Staff along with Parents who want to provide a better quality of life for black boys.

**By
Ajuma Muhammad**

Cover Design by Elaine Young
Book Editing by Professor Charles Wartts, BA, MFA
Typesetting/Layout by Sean R. Muhammad
(PK Publishing)

Printed in the United States of America
ISBN 978-0-9910578-1-8

"We must educate ourselves and our children into the power of knowledge which has elevated every people who have sought and used it.

We must give the benefit of our knowledge to the elevation of our own people."

~ Hon. Elijah Muhammad ~

WARNING

Explosive! This book is designed to move you toward action. If you're inclined to read this book and put it back on the shelf, then you probably shouldn't be reading this book. If you passively want change and don't want to be a change agent or an active participant in changing the present reality of where black boys find themselves, then you probably shouldn't be reading this book.

If you're reading this book and expecting others to do what you have the capacity to do, then you probably shouldn't be reading this book. If you think that the crisis facing black boys in America is hopeless and beyond repair, then you probably shouldn't be reading this book. If you think that there is a deliberate and concerted effort by America to <u>not</u> incarcerate, exploit, dumb down, subjugate and annihilate black boys—by any means necessary—then you probably shouldn't be reading this book.

If you think that black boys are prone to violence, destined to be criminals and are innately unfit to govern themselves, then you probably shouldn't be reading this book.

However, if you believe in the African proverb that "it takes a village to raise a child," then you're reading the right book.

If you believe that through community cooperation, economic self-sufficiency, African-centered education, and dedicated mentoring that we can empower black boys, then you're reading the right book. If you believe that good parenting starts at home and that parents should set the example of being their child's role model, then you're reading the right book.

If you believe that we have a duty to our ancestors to be great and to help our fallen brother or sister, then you're reading the right book. If you believe that we're destined to be great and have the capacity to do great things that stem from our black historical past, then you're reading the right book.

If you believe that we should define ourselves regardless of what others may think or feel about us, then you're reading the right book. If you believe that the leader that you're looking for is within you, then you're reading the right book.

If you believe that the next racial profiling victim to be slaughtered could be your son, cousin, nephew or family member, then you're reading the right book. If you believe that your input, activities and actions can help fashion a better life for black boys through mentoring, tutoring, parenting and being of great service to the black community, then you're reading the right book.

If you're willing to make a difference in the lives of black boys, then you should continue reading the prevention and intervention strategies noted in this book. Your job is to read this book and begin working toward immediate implementation of these concepts. After reading it, the book should be passed on to others so that they may benefit from these strategies.

May the God above bless you in all of your endeavors to empower black boys!

Dedication

This book is dedicated to the ancestors for paying the ultimate price with their lives. Words are not adequate to express the accolades due to them for allowing me the opportunity to be able to express myself, without reprisal, through the words in this book.

This book is also dedicated to the following:
My mother, Beatrice Hudson, my lovely wife Ajanna Muhammad; also, my children Ishmael Muhammad, Danielle Moore, Dawanna Moore and Davione Moore.

People who have inspired me over the years...

Hon. Elijah Muhammad	Verge "Bro. Sage" Gilliam
Min. Louis Farrakhan	Uncle Calvin Perkins
Dr. Robert L. Williams	Dr. Na'im Akbar
Bro. Anthony Shahid	Bro. Sultan Muhammad
Mrs. Lores Wells	Mr. Donald Wells
Dr. Dorothy Smith	Dr. Patrick Stack
Malcolm X	Dr. Jawanza Kunjufu
Bro. Akbar Muhammad	Dr. Khallid Muhammad

Foreword By

Dr. Robert L. Williams

It is easier to raise a strong child than it is to repair a broken man.

~ Frederick Douglass

The Black male has been on the radar in many ways for the last 40 or 50 years. Much has been written about the weaknesses and the problems of Black males but not much about their strengths, and very little about how to prevent or repair problems of the Black male.

As a "How-To" book, 101 Proven and Effective Strategies for Empowering Black Boys provides a set of practical guidelines for raising Black males.

The unpleasant reality is that far too many of our Black males are incarcerated, perhaps to some extent because of poor parenting. It is now time for us to stand up and meet the challenge. This book is a jump-start in that direction.

Ajuma Muhammad presents the development of four major child-rearing techniques for Black boys. They are:

(1) Strategies (2) Prevention

(3) Intervention and 4) Empowering

- Strategies are a carefully devised set of plans aimed at reaching a goal. Strategies move parents from "playing it by ear" techniques to having clearly developed plans for raising their boys.

- Prevention is another important technique that refers to an action taken to stop something before it occurs, as for example a serious misdemeanor or a crime of some sort.

- Intervention is a specific action taken to change what is happening or might happen especially in order to prevent something undesirable. Thus, this is a book of strategies for SOS (Saving Our Sons).

- Empowering refers to helping the Black male gain a sense of self-confidence, and to achieve rather than become an unfortunate statistic or "dead beat." Empowering is a goal of providing the individual with the resources or opportunities to reach a desired goal.

Ajuma Muhammad's 101 Prevention and Intervention Strategies are carried out via scripts or clear and concise statements for kids to live by. A script is a set of messages that parents give their kids.

Boys need to be scripted by their parents and parents need to know how to script their children properly. The boys should be taught proverbs, anecdotes, parables and humor. A story my stepfather taught me kept me out of prison.

He told the story about an Arkansas Correction Officer at Cummins Prison Farm who could stack three bricks, one on top of the other, hit the top brick with a huge belt and burst the brick on the bottom.

This story frightened me so much because I felt that if the officer would hit me on my butt, he would tear my insides out. I kept out of trouble because I certainly did not want to get into trouble and be sentenced to Cummins Prison Farm.

One last point must be mentioned. Although I have talked primarily about parents raising Black boys, this book is all-inclusive. Relatives, friends, teachers, counselors, psychotherapists, psychologists and social workers must also apply its principles. As the axiom states, "It takes a village to raise a child."

Robert L. Williams, PhD
Professor Emeritus
Washington University
August 17, 2013

"Birds teach birds how to fly. Fish teach fish how to swim. Black men must teach Black boys how to become responsible men."

"Real Black men are responsible, loving fathers who spend quality time with their children."

~ Ajuma Muhammad ~

"The ruin of a nation begins in the home of its people."
~ Ashanti Proverb ~

"You must structure your world so that you are constantly reminded of who you are."
~ Na'im Akbar ~

Introduction

The African-American community is in "deep trouble" with countless numbers of black boys failing in the society. You would have to be living under a rock to not know that black boys are failing in ways that are profoundly despicable.

Scores of them are failing on multiple fronts that threaten their very existence and future generations to come. Social forces continue to impact them daily although these social forces deny their impact and lay claim to not being complicit in the demise and destruction of young black boys. Social and psychological forces include but are not limited to the following:

- Satanically driven and seductive rap music and the so-called artist/clowns that perform this demeaning music.
- Video games that dominate the minds of our black boys by glamorizing violence and brutality.
- An unemployment rate that is twice the national average in the black community.
- Disproportionate legal system that favors one group over the other because of their financial resources and the color of their skin.
- Failing school systems throughout the country that maintain low expectations for black boys.
- Educational institutions that lack diversity and that are in denial about the value of culture and its relevance to empowering black boys.
- Deteriorating neighborhoods that create a psychological condition of hopelessness.
- Emerging immigrants that invade the black community and exploit it economically by not reinvesting their resources.

- Influx of gang activity and the collateral damage that it causes to those who participate and to those who don't.
- Lack of fathers in the home and the absence of men as positive role models. Shame on absent fathers for being a sperm donor and a coward.
- The psychological establishment that misdiagnoses black boys and falsely labels them while placing them on psychotropic drugs.
- Evangelical or religious leaders who teach doctrines that undermine personal initiative and self-reliance in our community. This keeps African-Americans emotionally high yet economically impotent while such religious organizations continue to enrich themselves with worldly goods.
- Not reporting crimes in our communities because many feel that such reporting is "snitching." The lack of reporting typically results in the onlooker being the next crime victim.

There is hope but it requires real men to commit themselves to real change in order to move black boys beyond the impasse they now find themselves in. There is an axiom that says, "Don't talk about it – be about it."

We have too much talking and too little action happening in the black community. It's time out for another meeting. We must teach our children to have a black perspective and to think in ways to empower other African-Americans who might also be struggling. Our children should know the story of young Emmett Till; Sean Bell of New York; and Trayvon Martin, followed by the countless number of black boys who were murdered for simply being in the wrong place at the wrong time.

We must become fathers to our children and teach them a better way of life, including how to become successful. There is no substitute for good parenting and being the primary role model in your child's life. As black men we should opt to be role models who are committed to the salvation of our black boys; nor should we abandon our black girls since they need father figures too.

Girls learn how to interact with other men by watching the example of their fathers. We must prioritize the things that matter the most by spending quality time with our children while helping them to chart their pathway in life. These concepts are incredibly effective when put into practice and devastating when they are not.

How long will we sit idly by while others build up their communities, thereby forging a positive reality for themselves? How long will we marvel at their feats when we have the same ability as African-American people to do these things ourselves? How long will we participate in our own economic genocide by not supporting black businesses? How long will we remain ignorant and inactive in our own community when we see clear evidence that rampart crime and other problems exist?

The problem with the aforementioned hurdles is that as a community we are running out of time. The clock is ticking and is about to reach its final tock!

The leader that you're looking for is within you! You must say, "If it is to be then it is up to me!" If you do not take that kind of dedicated stand, then the status quo will remain the same and dismal results compounded by collateral damage will surely follow for generations to come.

Why I wrote this book

I wrote this book to offer hope to those individuals who seriously and desperately want to empower our black boys. This book provides 101 powerful prevention and intervention strategies that have the potential to circumvent the seemingly inevitable tide of black male genocide currently taking place in America.

These strategies can be implemented by anyone regardless of color, but preferably a person of color should be the one taking the initiative to foster change in our black boys. The strategies put forth in this book represent no particular order, however each one of them is relevant and critical to the survival and success of black boys.

I was personally blessed years ago to be impacted by the teachings of the Hon. Elijah Muhammad and the Nation of Islam who taught the original history of the black man and his innate greatness. Upon being introduced to this history, I was then set forth on a journey that would enable me to impact over 30,000 youth through an organization I founded called The Association of African-American Role Models. This organization impacted the lives of thousands of youth for approximately twenty years.

Many who participated in the organization credit it for being the catalyst or turning point in their lives where they began to see the value and the God force within. Their lives were dramatically altered in a way that allowed them to be a shining beacon of hope and a change agent for others by applying this newfound knowledge.

With the aid and support of a dedicated cadre of brothers and sisters, this organization made a difference in the lives of countless numbers of black youth who had lost their way but are now on the road to redemption. These youth have been empowered to love their black selves and now see the greatness from within that was stolen from them through the smoke screen called the "American Educational System."

According to Dr. Carter G. Woodson, the American education system, with all of its defects, still has the power to extol Europeans while debasing the American Negro i.e., African-Americans, thereby robbing them of any substance that would allow them to see value in themselves.

He states that the Black man's history has been quietly removed or altered from the history books in such a way that it has rendered him an enemy to himself. Malcolm X once said that to teach a man to hate himself is worst than teaching him to hate someone else. The American educational system has taught the black man to hate himself without him even realizing it.

This book offers practical prevention and intervention strategies for the segment of our community deemed lost and unsalvageable by most experts in this society. Our black boys have the ability to turn their lives around given the right body of knowledge placed before them in addition to the people designated as role models who interact with them daily.

There is hope for the black community through self-awareness, community cooperation, identification of the enemy, economic interaction and commerce with each other followed by a willingness to serve those who look like us. It's time out for great speeches.

It's time out for the "whooping and hollering" that we too often find in our churches. Our most urgent task is to address the issue of how we as black people or African-Americans choose to define ourselves.

We must not allow others to define us. We must not expect handouts or sympathy for our plight although others are chiefly responsible for placing us there. There must be a concerted or unified effort by people of color to love ourselves in a way that allows us to support our fallen or struggling comrades.

Many of us seem to have forgotten where we've come from. Many of us seem to have forgotten the ancestors and the civil rights leaders who marched, bled and died for us to enjoy the social liberties that many of us take for granted today.

Shame on us for our ignorance and lack of appreciation for those who came before us! It is these, our heroes and heroines, who have made it possible for us to have the opportunities that we enjoy today. There is an axiom that says, "Those who fail to learn the lessons of history are doomed to repeat the same mistakes over and over again."

I pray that this book can offer insight and direction to anyone who is serious about the empowerment of black males in America. It is a practical guidebook that has the capability of correcting many of the social, spiritual, economic and environmental forces that are destructive in shaping our black boys.

Marcus Garvey once said, "Up you mighty race, you can accomplish what you will." Reading this book is not an accident. It was meant for you to pick up this book. Now what will you do with it? Knowledge is only powerful when applied and put into practice. If you read this book and do nothing with it then you should never have picked it up.

Will the realities of black life—racial profiling, disparity in the legal system, and the countless number of structural forces designed to immobilize African-Americans—only be taken to heart by you when your child, son, family member or someone that you know becomes a victim of racist America, i.e., young Trayvon Martin? The opportune time to act is always now!

"Up you mighty nation, you can accomplish what you will."
~ Marcus Garvey ~

101 Proven and Effective Strategies
for Empowering Black Males

For Counselors, Social Workers, Teachers, Administrators and other Support Staff along with Parents who want to provide a better quality of life for black boys.

"The major premise of effective education must be 'self-knowledge'. In order to achieve the goals of identity and empowerment, the educational process must be one that educes the awareness of who we are. This is not anything that's terribly mystical or complex. It really makes intuitive sense about what education should be." *Na'im Akbar*

The strategies provided below represent no particular order, however each one of them is essential to the reformation and transformation of black males in order that they might maximize their God-given internal talents to create a better future for themselves.

1. Maintain high expectations for young black males regardless of their personal and family situation. Be persistent and demand excellence. Let them know that they can overcome any adverse situation and that they should be optimistic about their future even when those around them may not be so supportive. (Prevention and intervention)

2. Request that they get academic tutoring if necessary to improve their grades. (Intervention)

3. Encourage parents or guardians to secure a psychological evaluation to determine the child's mental state and level of cognitive functioning. Many black boys are in need of

psychological counseling to better understand why their fathers are not in their life or in the home. They should be made to understand that their personal pain could be a source of motivation to help break the cycle of fatherlessness that is so prevalent in many black households. (Intervention)

4. Request parental involvement and participation when the child's behavior goes astray. Discuss proactive ways to modify the child's behavior with emphasis on verbal affirmation when the child is not in compliance. Implement a behavior modification program where the child is able to visually see his success with a behavior chart. (Intervention)

5. Request or require that black youngsters wear a "shirt and tie" at least one day a week in order to encourage a positive self-image. This will help them to see themselves in a business light as well as to better appreciate their potential and worth in the real world. (Prevention and Intervention)

6. Suggest to a parent or guardian that the student should receive individual psychological counseling outside of school in order to address unresolved issues. In such cases a black male therapist would be preferable. (Intervention)

7. Request a genogram, which enables one to pinpoint hereditary tendencies and recurring psychological patterns within the family structure. This dynamic tool can be used by an outside therapist to better understand the family's physical and psychological makeup

i.e., father, mother, siblings, foster parent, grandparents, etc. (Intervention)

8. Suggest family therapy as a viable alternative toward helping the family to be on one accord as they work through their issues and challenges. (Intervention)

9. Provide the family with a community resource guide or listing of the various community-based resources that include community programs, employment opportunities, educational information, counseling and tutoring aid, and possible male leadership programs.
(Prevention and Intervention)

10. Use the Occupational Outlook Handbook to make young black males aware of the opportunities available to them as well as to share information about possible career options. (Prevention)

11. Provide or create job-shadowing experiences for black boys in order to give them an insider's perspective into the world of work. This unique opportunity will help to motivate and shape their attitudes about the workplace. (Prevention)

12. Encourage black boys to get involved in a community project where they can be exposed to the various services and programs within their community. This experience will help them to be more connected to their community and to take pride in it by helping others. It also teaches them to be of service to others instead of

thinking only about themselves. (Prevention and Intervention)

13.   Identify a mentor in the community who can provide guidance and direction for black boys or perhaps become a mentor yourself. Mentors should spend quality time with black boys on a regular basis and discuss life issues with them while providing hope and encouragement. Activities can include sporting events, community programs, library, etc. (Intervention)

14.   Display empathy and not sympathy to our black boys by giving them high praise and positive affirmation on a daily basis even when they don't appear to be receptive to it. (Prevention and Intervention)

15.   Boys to Men Programs should be implemented in all schools where black boys are enrolled. While boys from other ethnic groups should be welcomed, the focus should be on black boys and their unique issues. These programs should include information on black inventors and achievers as well as relevant information about the plight and challenges of black males. (Prevention and Intervention)

16.   Encourage participation in sports or some other school-based activity, organization or program. This may include the debate team, chess club, band, public speaking, peer helper group, football, basketball, etc.…(Prevention and Intervention)

17.   Black boys should be recognized during "Pep Rallies" for their citizenship, academic

achievements, community service through volunteering, and other notable feats that increase their overall self-esteem and sense of self-worth. (Prevention)

18. Develop a Big Brother Program within the school so that each "big brother" is assigned a younger brother to mentor and guide during the school day. The responsibility of the "big brother" is to make sure that the younger brother has emotional support and direction as the latter strives to find his direction. (Prevention and Intervention)

19. Peer Helper Programs are highly beneficial. Therefore, black boys should participate in such programs or their school should initiate one if none exist. Peer Helper Programs are effective in that they allow students who might be experiencing a crisis to go to a trained peer to discuss their issues. Peer Helpers should also be trained in crisis management and diversion alternatives in order to address negative situations as they arise. (Intervention)

20. Schools should initiate a monthly lecture series where professional members of the community are able to speak directly with black boys as a means of acquainting them with career options and providing encouragement, thereby giving them hope. (Prevention)

21. Schools should initiate field trips that revolve around historically black colleges, learning about black culture in a particular city, and visiting a black business where they can meet

and dialogue with other black professionals. (Prevention)

22. School officials, counselors and school administrators should strongly encourage black boys to consider attending a historically black college because of their nurturing environment and the exposure to a history and vision of academic excellence and achievement, thereby instilling confidence to compete with others. (Prevention and Intervention)

23. Counselors, social workers and school administrators should identify and consider taking "at-risk" black boys to a "Scared Straight" program or exposing them to someone who has been incarcerated who can speak to black boys about the horrors of going to prison. This could serve as a deterrent to inappropriate behavior within the school. Emphasis should be placed on positive decision-making and career choices that lead to success. (Intervention)

24. Employ feature film and video assignments as therapy to reach out to black boys. Many boys are video-minded or visually oriented and learn best this way. Hard-hitting biographical films and other relevant presentations can be used effectively to bridge the gap between academic study and everyday reality.

Films such as The Antoine Fisher Story featuring Denzel Washington; Men of Honor, featuring Cuba Gooding, Jr.; and Something the Lord Has Made featuring Mos. Def. have the ability to inspire and motivate black boys to overcome the odds in their own lives. (Prevention and Intervention)

25. Encourage black boys to do weekly biography reports about black historical figures, inventors and achievers. Have them to demonstrate and share their knowledge at a school assembly or in the classroom so other students can learn vicariously. (Prevention)

26. Encourage all black boys to learn chess and to be a part of the school's debate team. If there is no chess club or debate team then start one. (Prevention and Intervention)

27. Encourage and demand accountability through consistency, hard work, dedication and focus. Demand accountability without excuses. Encourage self-inventory and self-reflection when black boys fall short of their goals. They should take ownership of their issues and be challenged to be empowered in order to move forward in their development. (Intervention)

28. Demonstrate "tough love" through consistency, fairness and by confronting our black boys when their effort or behavior falls short of their capability to succeed in the classroom and in life. (Intervention)

29. Recruit black men from professional circles such as policemen, firemen, lawyers, etc. to speak to black boys on a regular basis about life choices and to provide mentoring for them in their spare time if possible. (Prevention and Intervention)

30. Recruit more black males as teachers in the American school system. Less than two percent of the teachers in the American school system are black males. Over eighty percent are middle class white women, twelve percent middle class white males, and six percent black females. (Prevention and Intervention)

31. Recruit more black male counselors into the school system. Less than one percent of the counselors and social workers in the American school system are black men. Black boys tend to relate better and more effectively to black male therapists. (Prevention and Intervention)

32. Black boys should experience and be a part of a "Rites of Passage Ceremony" that speaks to academic and cultural attainment. These programs give them confidence and the self-worth necessary to develop and maintain a cultural worldview of themselves. Such programs can be implemented within the school system. (Prevention and Intervention)

33. Counselors, social workers and administrators should make home visits to their students in order to better understand their circumstances and to learn how to deal with them.

     This will give them a deeper connection and establish a positive rapport with all parties involved in the care and development of the black child. (Intervention)

34. Black boys should be confronted with their inconsistencies in a direct, gentle but loving

way in order to promote growth and development. There is nothing wrong with constructive criticism designed to empower. Black boys need discipline and will respond appropriately if presented in a stern yet respectful manner. (Intervention)

35. Counselors, social workers and school administrators should develop and create forums where black boys can voice their opinions and receive feedback; this helps to validate their concerns. Such a forum helps them to feel like a valued member of an institution that legitimately cares about them. (Prevention)

36. Field trip escorts and room fathers should be used to offer guidance to black boys when activities are presented at the school. This creates a broader spectrum of school unity, adoptive parent cooperation and positive educational interaction. (Prevention)

37. Acknowledge the presence of non-professional personnel such as black custodians and lunchroom staff along with safety officers as viable role models who are able to provide direction for black boys.

This expands the authority within a school, giving other school personnel leverage to provide guidance to our black boys. Each adult member of a school should have the designated authority to provide positive modeling and support for students through verbal enrichment. (Prevention and Intervention)

38. Instill and encourage the concept of black boys being self-disciplined as well as demonstrating positive self-restraint and good decision-making as the basis for achieving their goals. This can be accomplished through a daily "motto" or pledge that black boys read aloud each day before starting their classes. This creates positive reinforcement and positive expectations for black boys. (Prevention)

39. Counselors, social workers and administrators should use daily school events as "teachable moments" to provide didactic education to black boys about leadership and what it means to be a man. This can be accomplished through community assemblies, role-playing and skits, focus groups, and by having parents share their life experiences. (Prevention and Intervention)

40. Encourage higher education via college and trade schools as positive career options for black boys to pursue. Many black students have never had an opportunity to visit a college or trade school. Expose them to the various trade schools within their geographical area. See if there is a possibility that they could spend a day on a college campus or at a trade school where they can interact with students and ask questions about their experiences. (Prevention and Intervention)

41. Encourage black boys to participate in after school programs where they can receive tutoring or engage in enrichment activities

designed to build self-esteem and self-worth. (Prevention and Intervention)

42.   Increase black boys' exposure to technology via the Internet i.e., Skype, Facebook, Twitter etc. with the goal of learning how to wield the tools of entrepreneurship, business and commerce. Students should also learn to employ YouTube as a visual research medium for cultural enrichment, for learning about great black leaders, as well as a means of exploring their ancestral connection to Africa.

This will increase their knowledge and awareness of what it means to be a black male in America. As an alternative pursuit, they can learn how to build and repair computers as a way of generating income if they are too young to qualify for legal employment. (Prevention and Intervention)

43.   School administrators, counselors and social workers should promote smaller class sizes because it means less distractions and more personal attention that black boys can receive, thereby increasing their self-esteem and academic development.

They should also consider having all male classes, which also means fewer distractions. Having girls in the classroom with teenage boys frequently tends to complicate the learning process because of the natural attraction to the opposite sex. (Prevention and Intervention)

44.   Black boys must be taught to understand who they are from an historical and cultural

context. This can be achieved by having them develop pictorial collages where they cut pictures out of magazines that best represent their future in ten years.

These projects can consist of pictures of positive black women, positive black men or anecdotes, proverbs or parables that draw a connection to God so that they develop a God-consciousness as well as sensitivity to the plight of others. Each one of these projects is designed to empower the black boy internally, thereby making him feel good about himself and his community. (Prevention and Intervention)

45. Black boys must have an African-centered cultural identity in order to have a foundation upon which to stand. This gives them confidence in their race and their ability to compete on a higher level. Scores of media images and Hollywood portrayal of black males speak to the critical need for them to develop an African-centered identity.

This will ensure that when they become successful men they will maintain a sensitive connection to their communities by giving back rather than abandoning them. This can be achieved by doing research projects on Africa and learning about the great Kings and Queens that brought civilization to the world. (Prevention)

46. Classroom instruction must be culturally relevant, culturally appropriate, and culturally responsive to black boys in the classroom. Students rarely learn anything positive about Africa and only gain exposure

during Black History Month about some black achievers. This can be achieved through cultural education and by highlighting the enormous contributions that Africa and African-Americans have made to all of the sciences throughout the history of America. (Prevention)

47. Culturally responsive instruction should be occurring in all classrooms. According to Asa Hilliard, Professor of Educational Psychology and a noted African scholar, learning about one's history does not mean that one is prejudiced or discriminatory against other races or ethnic groups. It is important that black boys learn about their history and culture because it has the ability to empower them, thereby creating self-respect and respect for others. (Prevention)

48. Black boys should be encouraged to recite and remember the poem "Our Greatest Fear" by Marianne Williamson or another appropriate poem, proverb or quotation that can be read aloud daily. This pledge to themselves will remind them of their greatness and what they should be working towards. (Prevention)

49. Black boys should be encouraged to develop a pictorial montage of their life in ten years and use it as a visual and daily reminder of what they can achieve through hard work and focus. This will serve as visual stimulation and momentum to continue pursuing their dreams. This pictorial montage should be posted on the door of their bedroom or in plain view for others to see so that they too can "buy in" to the idea

of what the black child is working towards. (Prevention)

50. Black boys should be taught conflict resolution and the positive coping skills necessary to effectively deal with peer pressure and other social challenges. This will enable them to deal with the social forces that work against their achievements and aspirations. (Intervention)

51. Black boys should be allowed to work through many of their own issues without parental involvement and influence. Too many parents foster weakness and co-dependency by attempting to rescue their "baby boys" from dealing with any kind of adversity. Working through challenges will ultimately give black boys the self-confidence to work through their own issues when parental aid may not be available. (Parental Prevention)

52. Black boys should have to "work off" their punishment for being placed in In-School Suspension (ISS) or other forms of school detention should they occur. There is no reason for troubled students to make a serious change in their behavior if they're going to get a slap on the wrist. Having to clean up the school building or perform other manual labor is a more effective deterrent than ISS where kids tend to play and socialize all day. (Intervention)

53. Black boys should spend less time watching and playing video games, particularly the violent ones. They should spend more time reading and playing games that involve

critical thinking skills such as the following: checkers, chess, scrabble and other mentally challenging games.

Also, an educational alternative like studying a foreign language with flash cards is much more beneficial than playing mindless video games. Black boys spend less time on homework and studying than any other ethnic group. (Parental Intervention)

54. Black boys should have their homework reviewed by a parent or guardian for the sake of continuity and accountability. This system will also reinforce high academic expectations and discipline with regard to the student's work habits. (Parental Prevention)

55. Parents should not choose but should always monitor the friends of their sons. Good kids do bad things when bad kids surround them. Choosing good friends who share a similar value system is critical to the success of black boys in navigating the challenges of the world. (Parental Prevention)

56. Parents should talk to their black boys about the harmful effects of drugs as well as warn them about those who would try to convince them to sell drugs. They should cite the countless examples of black men who are incarcerated without the possibility of parole due to the Three Strikes Rule for selling drugs.

Discuss ways for them to walk away from those who would have them sell drugs without looking like a "punk." Always bear in mind that maintaining their confidence and "manhood" among their peers is essential to surviving and living another day. (Parental Prevention and Intervention)

57.   Parents should talk to their black boys about sexual abstinence and learning how to say no when confronted with peer pressure.

Teenage boys who abstain from sex are often viewed by their peers as "scared, soft, or a punk." Parents should teach their black boys about the negative and lasting consequences associated with teen pregnancy, STDs, HIV as well as many other problems that result from premature sex.

Parents should also talk to their black boys about the need to use protection such as a condom if they absolutely feel compelled to go out and have sex. A condom will reduce the chances of the girlfriend getting pregnant or the transmission of diseases. (Parental Prevention and Intervention)

58.   Parents should demand that their black boys attend some type of religious service weekly to enhance their relationship with God.

They should be attending the Mosque, Church, Synagogue or some kind of religious house where they are able to learn humility and the value of having good character.

They should not be given the option of staying at home and playing video games or hanging out with their friends. (Parental Prevention)

59.   Parents should give their black boys daily and weekly chores to complete in a timely manner. Hard work builds character, and there is no substitute for it. Hard work also teaches them the value of a dollar. It helps them to better understand the sacrifices that are made on their behalf by their parents. In addition, it drives home the message that hard work and good character will enable them to go far in realizing their life goals. (Parental Prevention)

60.   Parents should neither bargain nor pay their black boys to do chores around the house. These boys live in the same house and should not be paid for the entitlements that come from the sacrifices made on their behalf by their hardworking parents.

Rather, they should be made aware of how blessed they are to have a home when so many others are homeless at this time.

Parents should make their black boys take responsibility for the upkeep of their home (if they're fortunate enough to have one) by making sure that the house is clean and in good order at all times, including their bedrooms. (Parental Prevention)

61.   Parents should create opportunities for black boys to earn money as opposed to giving them money simply because they ask for it. Boys need to be taught what it means to be independent and what it means to be an entrepreneur.

In the summer time, they can make money by cutting grass or even washing cars; in winter by shoveling snow; and in the fall by raking leaves. Teach them that they have the ability to earn as much money as their heart desires by getting up off of their "duffs" and working hard. (Prevention and Intervention)

62. Parents should lead by example and let that be the best testimony of how they want their black boys to act and ultimately become. Their example will speak volumes in the years to come and will continue to have impact beyond anything that they may tell their black boys about life. My late great mentor, Mrs. Lores Wells, would always tell me, "I would rather see a sermon than to hear a sermon any day." (Parental Prevention)

63. Parents should have their black boys do daily and weekly book reports on the black experience, starting with the great Kings and Queens of Africa. Then encourage them to present their report before other family members who should be joining in and celebrating the presentation. This will give young boys a thorough understanding of their history and culture, thereby creating a solid cultural foundation. (Parental Prevention)

64. Parents should turn off all electronic devices daily, or no less than twice a week, and insist upon having dinner together as a family. The dinner table presents a rare opportunity to spend time face-to-face as well as discuss events pertaining to the family or the world in general. This creates a sense of cohesiveness and family togetherness. All too often members of the family now eat in

their bedrooms while watching TV when they should unite around the dinner table. (Prevention and Intervention)

65. Black boys should be encouraged to demonstrate eye contact as a way of communicating their thoughts. All too often black boys communicate by looking away or looking down when communicating with others. This behavioral change will enhance their ability to communicate effectively and poignantly to the person that they are speaking with. (Prevention and Intervention)

66. Black boys should be encouraged to deliver a strong and firm handshake when encountering others. This handshake in the world of business and in other circles communicates a statement of confidence and assurance. These intangible yet essential gestures go a long way in making a statement about one's self. (Prevention and Intervention)

67. Black boys should be permitted and encouraged to speak for themselves without their parents trying to speak for them. Nothing is worst than when a teacher or counselor asks a black boy about this or that and the parent automatically assumes the role of spokesperson for their son. Let them speak and think for themselves without parental involvement. They cannot learn to be independent thinkers and speakers if their parents are always speaking for them. (Prevention)

68. Parents should be consistent when dispensing punishment to their black boys for errant behavior.

Parents often say one thing and do another, which sends a mixed message to their son. Some parents go back and forth with punishment for a particular misdeed, which suggests that the punishment is only a punishment if the parent is in a bad mood. Punishments should be carried out to the full extent of what was determined beforehand or what has been agreed upon. (Intervention)

69. School officials during Black History Month should encourage black boys to go over and beyond their understanding of learning about Black History Month.

They should encourage the following: role playing and skits, plays, dramatizations, spoken word experiences, and bringing in outside guests to provide insight about some of their life experiences and how they were able to be successful in spite of adversity. (Prevention and Intervention)

70. Black mothers need to be cautiously concerned about the character of the boyfriend, stepfather or male of interest who may potentially become a partner for them and their son. The quality of his character and example will speak volumes about the future unity of the family.

His example will either serve as a conduit for positive transformation into manhood or as a negative model that fosters wrong pathways into manhood. Placing the right kind of man in front of your son is critical to his success in life. (Prevention and Intervention)

71. Black mothers should understand that they cannot teach a boy to be a man. You can only provide for them and give them good guidance; however, you need a man to teach your son how to best become a man.

If there is any consolation to be offered to those women or mothers who might be offended by this critical message, know that a man cannot teach a young girl how to be a woman. Male and female psychology and orientation to life makes them different and unique individuals in their own right. (Prevention and Intervention)

72. School officials and parents should demand that black boys and others in the school and in the home interact with adults by saying "yes sir" and "no sir." Do not allow them to get away with saying "yeah" and "nah."

Good manners are essential when interacting with others in situations where behavioral protocol is expected. (Prevention and Intervention)

73. Parents should talk to their black boys about the concept of dating and marriage. They should discourage their black boys from falling into the "playboy" syndrome where it is fashionable to have twenty girlfriends at one time.

Black boys should be made aware of the fact that "the woman" (who is also their beloved mothers, sisters and grandmothers) is a blessing from God and should be treated with honor and respect.

Teach boys to have standards and that marriage is a sacred institution that requires a commitment to do the right thing. Teach them that the "marriage union" is an honorable thing.

Everyone deserves to have a positive marital model in front of them to act as a strong example to strive for as they become of age. (Parental Prevention)

74.   Parents should establish and define the word "manhood" and what it means to them. There should be some family marker or ceremony that the family uses to determine that the black boy has now become a man.

This will vary from family to family. Manhood should be based upon accountability, self-development and being responsible when it comes to doing the right thing.

Examples include a level of independence followed by an initiative to get things done without making excuses. Men make things happen or they find a way to get things done without excuses. (Prevention)

75.   School officials along with counselors, social workers, support staff and parents should discourage black boys from ever calling a black female (or any woman for that matter) a "bitch" or the B – Word.

The word in and of itself is despicable and doesn't represent the true essence of a woman as an active agent of God. Black boys should understand that every time they refer to a black female as a "bitch" that that makes them a "son of a bitch" since all of them were born from a woman. (Prevention)

76.   School officials along with counselors, social workers, support staff and parents should encourage black boys to never use the "N-Word" or call someone a "nigger" since the word is derogatory and was created by white people as a way of belittling or putting black people down.

        The word as currently "uploaded" into the consciousness and vocabulary of black boys via rap music and mass media effectively implants a template of dehumanization and degradation. We should refer to each other in more congenial terms like "Brother, Sister, King, Queen, Prince, etc. These culturally enriched terms create a sense of empowerment and motivation to achieve one's goals. (Prevention and Intervention)

77.   School officials along with counselors, social workers, support staff and parents should discourage black boys from ever wearing "sagging pants." Use issues of appropriate dress as "teachable moments" to provide education and understanding to those who would "sag" their pants.

        They should be made to understand that this kind of behavior originated from penal institutions and in no way represents positive and program minded individuals who desire higher goals in life.

Sagging pants shouldn't define your existence; however, it does represent a negative brand that falsely identifies many black males with "thug life" or criminal behavior.

Teach your students to pull up their pants and to represent themselves in a manner that is respectable and worthy of family honor. (Prevention and Intervention)

78.   Black boys should be taught to be defenders of their community by maintaining a watchful eye on those who seek to destroy their community.

They should be taught to become actively involved in local politics, vote on a regular basis, to clean up paper and trash wherever they might find it, and to take pride in their community. Communication, collaboration, commitment and consistency go a long way in making community residents feel safe and good about their neighborhood. (Prevention and Intervention)

79.   School officials along with counselors, social workers, support staff and parents should educate black boys about the "true purpose" of going to school.

They should be made to understand the seriousness and the value of education and how it has the ability to uplift and empower them. They need to understand that there are enemy forces in society that have been

38

designated to destroy them by "any means necessary"; only by developing a strong educational foundation will they acquire the necessary fortitude to counteract those forces.

They should be made to understand the critical role of education in transforming their lives. This means that they do not go to school to become the next "class clown" or play the dozens and be unproductive in every imaginable kind of way. Rather, they should be drilled on the importance of getting good grades and putting forth the maximum effort in achieving their educational goals. (Prevention)

80. Parents should educate and empower their black boys by teaching them never to seek or expect "something for nothing." Teach them to pay their own way for anything that they may desire in life and let them know that they are worthy and capable of accomplishing anything they set their minds on. Parents should provide high praise and words of encouragement for a job well done on a daily basis. (Prevention)

81. Parents should demand respect for all parental decisions from their black boys, even when the decision is not to the child's liking. Young men should learn to accept the word "no" and not take it as a personal attack when their requests are not granted. Black boys should understand that constructive criticism is designed to equip them with the internal fortitude necessary to make it through life. (Parental Prevention)

82. School officials along with counselors, social workers, support staff and parents should encourage black boys to be role models wherever they find themselves, but especially in their school and community.

Students should be made to understand that they have a personal and social obligation to render service to others based on the sacrifices that have been made on their behalf. They should cultivate an appreciation of the heroic sacrifices made by their ancestors who have paved the way for them to receive many of the social liberties that they now take for granted. (Prevention)

83. School officials along with counselors, social workers, support staff and parents should encourage black boys to maintain a positive attitude and disposition at all times.

Let them know that it's okay to get angry and upset sometimes; however, it is more important to develop self-control and to think through a situation rather than respond negatively.

Teach them the concept that "it's not what happens to you but how you choose to respond to it" that determines the ultimate outcome of all situations.

Teach them the long-term consequences of their decisions and how it impacts every aspect of their lives as well as those around them. (Prevention)

84. Parents should teach their black boys how to effectively deal with peer pressure, especially

when people start "hating" on them. They must understand that a verbal beat down or "playing the dozens" for many black boys is almost a rite of passage for becoming who they are.

These harsh verbal jabs start as early as pre-school and persists through elementary, middle school, and high school. Young men must understand how not to wear their feelings on their sleeves.

They need to understand that no matter how perfect or imperfect they may be, someone will find something negative to say about them. Peers typically tend to be "haters," particularly in the case of black boys who demonstrate a desire to excel in life.
Create role-playing scenarios at home that anticipate challenges on school premises and see how your son deals with the situation.

Discuss real-life conflicts and their reactions to them. Put them in perspective so that black boys will know how to effectively handle such situations when they arise, as they surely will at some point in time. (Prevention and Intervention)

85. Black parents should teach their boys to stand for a principle even if it means telling on someone (i.e., snitching) because by taking action they insure that the truth will prevail in that instance.

Dr. Martin L. King once said that a man who stands for nothing surely will fall for anything. Too many of our young black males are afraid to stand for truth and righteousness but seem more than willing to stand for foolishness.

The black community seems to have a schizophrenic mentality when a crime is perpetuated against one of their own and they need someone to stand on their behalf.

However, when someone else is victimized they are often missing in action or silent. We must remember that we can't have it both ways if we want our communities to be safe and empowered. (Prevention and Intervention)

86.   Black parents must teach their boys about the hypocrisy that exists in most black communities, beginning with the so-called "rap-artists" whom most teenagers tend to glorify.

Many of the rappers that black boys look up to are not fit to be called a role model or even an example of good character since strong community-centered values are often lacking.

Many rappers represent the worst examples for our youth to emulate. Many were former drug dealers and the worst that our community has produced. However, it should be said that not all rappers are bad examples to emulate. Some are really great people with a positive message for our young people, and these are the ones that should be listened to.

Parents and educators should educate young people about the differences and why positive rap is important for their development. (Prevention and Intervention)

87. School officials along with counselors, social workers, support staff and parents should encourage black boys to make good choices when it comes to their friends.

Selecting bad friends could prove detrimental to their health, life and overall well-being. Let them know that the choice of a good friend should reflect and reinforce the values and goals that they subscribe to.

Teach them discernment when it comes to friend selection and how to stay away from those so-called "friends" that may lead them astray.

Drill your young people with the axiom that the choice of a friend can have immeasurable consequences, both good and bad. (Prevention and Intervention)

88. School officials along with counselors, social workers, support staff and parents should encourage black boys to research and review the history of those students who have made it to professional rank in their given sport.

They need to know that seventy percent of the athletes who make it on the professional level often end up filing bankruptcy or losing the majority of their earnings because they relied on others to manage their money.

They need to know that a "gold brain" is better than a "gold chain" around your neck. Teach them that sports should be "viewed as

43

a means to an end" and that there is no substitute for education in attaining a quality future. (Prevention and Intervention)

89.   Parents should encourage their black boys to be empowered and not to depend on the use of a pill as a substitute for good decision-making and responsible behavior.

Encourage them to believe in themselves and teach them self-discipline in the home by observing their responses when they can't get their way or have been told "no" for something.

Use these experiences as "teachable moments" to instill discipline and "tough love." An experiment known as The Placebo Effect vividly illustrates how dependency is often a state of mind. In this case a multi-vitamin was substituted for "Risperdal, Seroquel, Ritalin, Concerta, Zoloft, Celexa, Welbutrin, and other anti-depressant drugs.

However, the participants who took the multi-vitamin or "placebo" experienced the same results as those taking the anti-depressants simply because they were told that the pill would make them better. Clients or patients taking these addictive drugs often see meager results if any, while the side effects are often debilitating and reprehensible.

Try the positive alternatives of consistent prayer, a daily commitment to homework, as well as a stable home environment supported by positive parental modeling and reinforcement as critical keys for modifying the behavior of black boys. (Prevention and Intervention)

90.   Black parents should make their boys feel special through daily words of encouragement followed by positive affirmation after completing household tasks or chores.

Keep them busy reading biographies of famous black leaders, inventors and those who have made meaningful contributions to the black struggle such as Malcolm X, Elijah Muhammad, Huey P. Newton, Paul Robeson, Jackie Robinson, etc.

The effect of such positive encouragement is exemplified by a scientific experiment involving monkeys who received milk from a wire frame monkey versus a monkey who didn't dispense milk but provided comfort through touch.

The baby monkeys were drawn to the warmth and physical contact of the monkey who provided care and concern despite the wire frame monkey that dispensed milk.

Black boys need a genuine and authentic connection to their parents in order to help them feel good about themselves. (Prevention and Intervention)

91.   "The Pygmalion Effect" is based upon teachers who taught a group of underachieving students but were told that these students were high achieving students. The result was that the "under achievers" performed at a higher academic level because

the expectations of their teachers were different.

Another group of teachers were told that their high achieving students were really low achievers, a perception which resulted in a lower academic output because their expectations were lower. Parents should have high academic expectations of their black boys, an attitude that goes hand in hand with academic accountability. (Prevention and Intervention)

92. "Learned Helplessness" is a term that was coined by a psychologist who applied electrical shocks to dogs who eventually internalized a sense of hopelessness and lack of response.

Many of our black boys have internalized a sense of "learned hopelessness" due to all the negative social and psychological forces around them.

As educators, parents, and activists we have to instill a sense of "learned optimism" in order to give black boys hope for the future. They should be surrounded by a cadre of people that love and want to protect them from the community vices that are waiting to tear them down.

They need positive parental images and consistent lifestyles that promote successful models of human development. (Prevention and Intervention)

93. The "Stockholm Syndrome" is based on the concept of the captive who takes the side of

the captor after being held for a long time in captivity.

This is equivalent to African-Americans who were held in captivity against their will in America for over three hundred years and have now taken on the identity of being an AMERICAN more so than being an African-American.

Ruth Shay once said, "When you don't know you have been spit upon, it doesn't matter what else you think you know."

This is important because black parents pass on to black boys the notion of being an AMERICAN and forget to emphasize the importance of being "Black in America."

This is critical because black males are often marginalized, stereotyped, and the object of persecution particularly when it comes to race and the penal system in America.

Information and awareness is powerful to our black boys and may make the difference between life and death. (Prevention and Intervention)

94.   Parents should work extra hard to eliminate white sugar from black boys' diets, and make sure that their boys have a healthy diet absent of junk foods and beverages loaded with sugar and sweeteners.

Sugar is a stimulant that has the capacity to make black boys hyperactive, thereby increasing the probability of them getting labeled ADD or ADHD by those who often want to categorize and ostracize them.

Feed young men healthy fruits and vegetables and make sure they get the proper amount of rest at night. (Prevention and Intervention)

95.   Black parents should not allow their boys to play video games unless they are educational, cultural or have some kind of academic benefit. Video games that dramatize killing, "rugged individualism," disrespect toward women, and random violence are deadly combinations for black boys.

Don't buy them or if you have them throw them out with the rest of the trash in your house. (Prevention and Intervention)

96.   Young black boys and black baby boys should not get their ears pierced because it takes the focus off their ability to enjoy the wonderful experience of just being a kid. Their focus as a young boy should be on education, discipline, manhood and discovering their true purpose in life.

When black boys get their ears pierced, a distracting attitude of trying to be "cool" or "cute" is interjected into their development that makes it more difficult to maintain their focus on the things that matter. (Prevention)

97.   "Birds of a feather flock together" is an axiom that says that people tend to surround themselves with others with whom they share a common interest.

Teach our black boys to surround themselves with other boys who are positive and desire to achieve something in life. Often time this particular decision can powerfully impact their future. If they choose negative peers to be around, the outcome is too often a tragic one. (Prevention and Intervention)

98.   The "Black Box" is another metaphor that highlights how the "Power of the Universe, The Wisdom of the Universe and The Knowledge of Creation" is really within our black boys. Once upon a time two Greek Gods were pondering where to put the little black box containing those essential powers listed above.

Most people believed that the little black box would be placed on the highest mountain or the deepest ocean, but later found out that the power that they sought was really within them. Teach our black boys that they have the power! (Prevention and Intervention)

99.   Parents and educators should teach and talk to black boys by using positive metaphors which have a powerful and lingering effect on them. People tend to remember stories rather than instructions or redirection.

A wise man once said when talking to a couple of youths who wanted to embarrass him before a public gathering, that the bird you hold in your hand depends on you for his survival—whether you choose to crush it or simply let it go. He told them that the bird is in your hands! (Prevention)

100. Parents should inspire their black boys to "leave a legacy" of honor and respect for future generations by being of service to others. Dr. Martin L. King once said that it didn't matter how long a man lived but what he did with the time that he was allowed.

One person can make a difference: Malcolm X, Nelson Mandela, Marcus Garvey, Noble Drew Ali, Rosa Parks and you if you choose to see their spirits inside of you. (Prevention)

101. Black parents must teach their boys about "The Urgency of Now," a concept that means having a clear plan of action about how they want to achieve their goals.

A goal without a plan is simply a wish. Black boys should be introduced to the aforementioned Occupational Outlook Handbook which details over four thousand different occupations and the process for achieving one's desired goal.

It is a wonderful book that highlights the education black boys will need to realize their aims followed by the nature of the job, licenses needed, a forecast for the future, etc. Knowledge is power if used correctly and strategically. (Prevention and Intervention)

Conclusion

Our children are failing in the most significant aspects of their lives. It is incumbent upon us to take a moment to reflect while asking ourselves, "What can I do to make a difference?"

Or what can I contribute that would alter the seemingly inevitable fate of our black boys who stand little chance of ever realizing their potential? You may raise such question internally or you may just decide, "It's not my problem."

Nonetheless, if you picked up this book there is still hope for our black boys. Anything and everything positive contributes to the redirection and empowerment of our black boys. You may want to consider developing a mentoring program in your neighborhood, volunteering as a tutor, spending quality time with your own children or family members. Just bear in mind that the time is now to be a change agent!

The time is now for serious minded individuals who really want to make a difference in the life of a black boy. Role models, mentors, father figures and caring individuals are wanted at any time to step into a position of leadership and make a difference in the life of a black child. Stop waiting on the government and benevolent white folks to liberate us – it's not going to happen.

Your present condition and status in America speaks to the unwillingness of White America and the government to resolve many of the social challenges imposed upon African-Americans, although they are responsible for putting so many of us in a wretched condition.

Your condition will change once the black community i.e., the Black man has decided enough is enough. Crime, lawlessness, mayhem and the chaotic lifestyles that many African-Americans find themselves in will change only when we decide to take our communities back by any means necessary.

If you read this book and decide to do nothing, then shame on you! It means that you are complicit or passively turning your back on your ancestors and those who fought to give you an opportunity to enjoy the social and economic benefits that you exercise today without fear of reprisals from those who would like to take those opportunities away from you.

Your inaction and passivity further cements a permanent place at the bottom for our black boys. Your excuse-making and cowardice is comparable to that of Benedict Arnold, a known traitor throughout American history. It means that you are inconsequential and that your passage through this life is meaningless. The law of nature says that in order to receive blessings you have to be a blessing to others.

I pray that God gives you the strength and the insight to do more and to re-commit yourself to the empowerment of black boys.

Our black boys are desperately seeking role models, father figures, and men who see the value in them regardless of the label that society has placed on them. It is incumbent upon us to be the change that we want to see if tomorrow is to be a brighter day for our black boys.

About the Author

Ajuma Muhammad is the Founder and Executive Director of Ajuma's Counseling Services, LLC, an agency whose mission is to empower young people and their families through individual and group counseling services designed to help them overcome some of their daily challenges.

Muhammad is also a nationwide motivational speaker and community activist, and his appeal is to anyone who is willing to listen and who has a genuine concern for youth and the community.

As a devoted husband and loving father of four adult children, he is dedicated to the uplift of the community through the empowerment of our youth. This he accomplishes through informational lectures, individual counseling, family therapy, positive modeling and by inspiring others to embrace the positive possibilities of life.

Muhammad has studied at several universities, receiving a Bachelor of Science Degree in Psychology and an Associate Degree in Child Development Technology from Central State University. He has also earned a Master of Arts degree in Counselor Education from the University of Missouri-St. Louis.

In addition, he has done graduate work toward his doctoral degree at Webster University, St. Louis University and the University of Missouri St. Louis. He now serves as a Licensed Psychotherapist in private practice who contracts with the State of Missouri Department of Children Services to provide mental health services to adolescents.

To his literary credit, Muhammad is the author of *Understanding the Crisis of the Black Male: A Handbook on Raising Black Boys to be Responsible Black Men.* He is currently working on Volume II of *Understanding the Crisis of the Black Male.*

As a Licensed Psychotherapist, Muhammad engages his audiences through experiential learning exercises designed to promote self-awareness, cultural enrichment, positive self-development and personal accountability. His goal is to empower his audience to move past "mental paralysis" to a more positive realm of human possibility by understanding one's true purpose and goals in life.

Muhammad's extensive travels have taken him throughout Africa, Europe, China, Latin America and the Caribbean where the opportunity to meet other people and learn about other cultures has enriched his perspective on life, love and being of service to others.

This enriching experience has allowed him to study, compare and contrast how life in America could be more plausible and poignant for those who are called by a higher purpose in life through service to others.

His style of motivating and encouraging his teenage audiences through humor, "Hip-Hop" lingo, and experiential learning exercises is highly effective. He is lauded for his tireless efforts in helping African-American teenagers to recognize and realize their unique talents and abilities. As one local writer states, "Muhammad has positively influenced the lives of more than 30,000 youth during his phenomenal career as a motivator—and that, in itself, is noteworthy."

References

- Akbar, N. 1984. Chains and Images of Psychological Slavery. Jersey City: New Mind Productions.

- Dubois, W. E. B. 1961. Souls of Black Folks. New York: Dodd, Mead & Co.

- Farrakhan, L. 1979-1996. The Final Call. Chicago, IL: Final Call Inc.

- Hilliard, A.G., III. 1998. SBA: The Re-awakening of the African mind. Gainesville, FL: Makare Publishing.

- Kunjufu, J. 1984. Developing Positive Self-Images and Discipline in Black Children. Chicago: African-American Images.

- Muhammad, E. 1965. Message to the Black Man. Chicago: Muhammad Mosque of Islam, No. 2

- Schott Foundation for Public Education, 2008. Given Half a Chance. The Schott 50- state reports on public education and black males. Retrieved from www.blackboysreport.org

- Wilson, A. 1990. Black-on-Black Violence: The Psycho-dynamics of Black Self-Annihilation in Service of White Domination. New York: Afrikan World Infosystems.

- Woodson, C.G. 1933. The Mis-Education of the Negro. Washington, DC: The Associated Publishers.

- Wright, B. 1986. The Psychopathic Racial Personality. Chicago: Third World Press.

This document was developed and created by its author Ajuma Muhammad, MA, Ed., LPC, BCPC and Licensed Psychotherapist

Available for Speaking Engagements
Visit:
www.ajuma.org

Or email us at:
Amuha14223@aol.com

CPSIA information can be obtained
at www.ICGtesting.com
Printed in the USA
FFOW02n0906130715
14952FF